THE BELFRY OF BRUGES

THE BELFRY OF BRUGES

BY

HENRY WADSWORTH LONGFELLOW

1845

This text was originally published in the United State
s in the year 1845
The text is in the public domain.

TABLE OF CONTENTS

Carillon 7
The Belfry of Bruges 11

MISCELLANEOUS 13

A Gleam of Sunshine 15
The Arsenal at Springfield 19
Nuremberg 21
The Norman Baron 25
Rain in Summer 29
To a Child 33
Occultation of Orion 39
The Bridge 43
To the Driving Cloud 47

SONGS 49

Seaweed 51
The Day is Done 53
Afternoon in February 55
To an Old Danish Song-book 57
Walter von der Vogelweide 61
Drinking Song 63
The Old Clock on the Stairs 65
The Arrow and the Song 69

SONNETS 71

The Evening Star 73
Autumn 75
Dante 77

TRANSLATIONS 79

The Hemlock-Tree 81
Annie of Tharaw 83
The Statue over the Cathedral Door 85
The Legend of the Crossbill 87
The Sea Hath its Pearls 89
Poetic Aphorisms: 91
- Money
- The Best Medicine
- Sin
- Poverty and Blindness
- Law of Life 92
- Creeds
- The Restless Heart
- Christian Love
- Art and Tact 93
- Retribution
- Truth
- Rhymes

Curfew 95

NOTES 97

ABOUT THE AUTHOR 105

CARILLON

In the ancient town of Bruges,
In the quaint old Flemish city,
As the evening shades descended,
Low and loud and sweetly blended,
Low at times and loud at times,
And changing like a poet's rhymes,
Rang the beautiful wild chimes
From the Belfry in the market
Of the ancient town of Bruges.

Then, with deep sonorous clangor
Calmly answering their sweet anger,
When the wrangling bells had ended,
Slowly struck the clock eleven,
And, from out the silent heaven,
Silence on the town descended.
Silence, silence everywhere,
On the earth and in the air,
Save that footsteps here and there
Of some burgher home returning,
By the street lamps faintly burning,
For a moment woke the echoes
Of the ancient town of Bruges.

But amid my broken slumbers
Still I heard those magic numbers,
As they loud proclaimed the flight
And stolen marches of the night;
Till their chimes in sweet collision
Mingled with each wandering vision,
Mingled with the fortune-telling
Gypsy-bands of dreams and fancies,
Which amid the waste expanses
Of the silent land of trances
Have their solitary dwelling;
All else seemed asleep in Bruges,
In the quaint old Flemish city.

And I thought how like these chimes
Are the poet's airy rhymes,
All his rhymes and roundelays,
His conceits, and songs, and ditties,
From the belfry of his brain,
Scattered downward, though in vain,
On the roofs and stones of cities!
For by night the drowsy ear
Under its curtains cannot hear,
And by day men go their ways,
Hearing the music as they pass,
But deeming it no more, alas!
Than the hollow sound of brass.

Yet perchance a sleepless wight,
Lodging at some humble inn
In the narrow lanes of life,
When the dusk and hush of night
Shut out the incessant din
Of daylight and its toil and strife,
May listen with a calm delight
To the poet's melodies,
Till he hears, or dreams he hears,
Intermingled with the song,
Thoughts that he has cherished long;
Hears amid the chime and singing
The bells of his own village ringing,
And wakes, and finds his slumberous eyes
Wet with most delicious tears.

Thus dreamed I, as by night I lay
In Bruges, at the Fleur-de-Blé,
Listening with a wild delight
To the chimes that, through the night,
Rang their changes from the Belfry
Of that quaint old Flemish city.

THE BELFRY OF BRUGES

In the market-place of Bruges stands the belfry old and brown;
Thrice consumed and thrice rebuilded, still it watches o'er the town.

As the summer morn was breaking, on that lofty tower I stood,
And the world threw off the darkness, like the weeds of widowhood.

Thick with towns and hamlets studded, and with streams and vapors gray,
Like a shield embossed with silver, round and vast the landscape lay.

At my feet the city slumbered. From its chimneys, here and there,
Wreaths of snow-white smoke, ascending, vanished, ghost-like, into air.

Not a sound rose from the city at that early morning hour,
But I heard a heart of iron beating in the ancient tower.

From their nests beneath the rafters sang the swallows wild and high;
And the world, beneath me sleeping, seemed more distant than the sky.

Then most musical and solemn, bringing back the olden times,
With their strange, unearthly changes rang the melancholy chimes,

Like the psalms from some old cloister, when the nuns sing in the choir;
And the great bell tolled among them, like the chanting of a friar.

Visions of the days departed, shadowy phantoms filled my brain;
They who live in history only seemed to walk the earth again;

All the Foresters of Flanders, mighty Baldwin Bras de Fer,
Lyderick du Bucq and Cressy, Philip, Guy de Dampierre.

I beheld the pageants splendid, that adorned those days of old;
Stately dames, like queens attended, knights who bore the Fleece of Gold;

Lombard and Venetian merchants with deepladen argosies;
Ministers from twenty nations; more than royal pomp and ease.

I beheld proud Maximilian, kneeling humbly on the ground;
I beheld the gentle Mary, hunting with her hawk and hound;

And her lighted bridal-chamber, where a duke slept with the queen,
And the armed guard around them, and the sword unsheathed between.

I beheld the Flemish weavers, with Namur and Juliers bold,
Marching homeward from the bloody battle of the Spurs of Gold;

Saw the fight at Minnewater, saw the White Hoods moving west,
Saw great Artevelde victorious scale the Golden Dragon's nest.

And again the whiskered Spaniard all the land with terror smote;
And again the wild alarum sounded from the tocsin's throat;

Till the bell of Ghent responded o'er lagoon and dike of sand,
"I am Roland! I am Roland! there is victory in the land!"

MISCELLANEOUS

A GLEAM OF SUNSHINE

This is the place. Stand still, my steed,
  Let me review the scene,
And summon from the shadowy Past
  The forms that once have been.

The Past and Present here unite
  Beneath Time's flowing tide,
Like footprints hidden by a brook,
  But seen on either side.

Here runs the highway to the town;
  There the green lane descends,
Through which I walked to church with thee,
  O gentlest of my friends!

The shadow of the linden-trees
  Lay moving on the grass;
Between them and the moving boughs,
  A shadow, thou didst pass.

Thy dress was like the lilies,
  And thy heart as pure as they:
One of God's holy messengers
  Did walk with me that day.

I saw the branches of the trees
    Bend down thy touch to meet,
The clover-blossoms in the grass
    Rise up to kiss thy feet,

"Sleep, sleep to-day, tormenting cares,
    Of earth and folly born!"
Solemnly sang the village choir
    On that sweet Sabbath morn.

Through the closed blinds the golden sun
    Poured in a dusty beam,
Like the celestial ladder seen
    By Jacob in his dream.

And ever and anon, the wind,
    Sweet-scented with the hay,
Turned o'er the hymn-book's fluttering leaves
    That on the window lay.

Long was the good man's sermon,
    Yet it seemed not so to me;
For he spake of Ruth the beautiful,
    And still I thought of thee.

Long was the prayer he uttered,
    Yet it seemed not so to me;
For in my heart I prayed with him,
    And still I thought of thee.

But now, alas! the place seems changed;
Thou art no longer here:
Part of the sunshine of the scene
With thee did disappear.

Though thoughts, deep-rooted in my heart,
Like pine-trees dark and high,
Subdue the light of noon, and breathe
A low and ceaseless sigh;

This memory brightens o'er the past,
As when the sun, concealed
Behind some cloud that near us hangs
Shines on a distant field.

THE ARSENAL AT SPRINGFIELD

This is the Arsenal. From floor to ceiling,
Like a huge organ, rise the burnished arms;
But front their silent pipes no anthem pealing
Startles the villages with strange alarms.

Ah! what a sound will rise, how wild and dreary,
When the death-angel touches those swift keys
What loud lament and dismal Miserere
Will mingle with their awful symphonies

I hear even now the infinite fierce chorus,
The cries of agony, the endless groan,
Which, through the ages that have gone before us,
In long reverberations reach our own.

On helm and harness rings the Saxon hammer,
Through Cimbric forest roars the Norseman's song,
And loud, amid the universal clamor,
O'er distant deserts sounds the Tartar gong.

I hear the Florentine, who from his palace
Wheels out his battle-bell with dreadful din,
And Aztec priests upon their teocallis
Beat the wild war-drums made of serpent's skin;

The tumult of each sacked and burning village;
The shout that every prayer for mercy drowns;
The soldiers' revels in the midst of pillage;
The wail of famine in beleaguered towns;

The bursting shell, the gateway wrenched asunder,
The rattling musketry, the clashing blade;
And ever and anon, in tones of thunder,
The diapason of the cannonade.

Is it, O man, with such discordant noises,
With such accursed instruments as these,
Thou drownest Nature's sweet and kindly voices,
And jarrest the celestial harmonies?

Were half the power, that fills the world with terror,
Were half the wealth, bestowed on camps and courts,
Given to redeem the human mind from error,
There were no need of arsenals or forts:

The warrior's name would be a name abhorred!
And every nation, that should lift again
Its hand against a brother, on its forehead
Would wear forevermore the curse of Cain!

Down the dark future, through long generations,
The echoing sounds grow fainter and then cease;
And like a bell, with solemn, sweet vibrations,
I hear once more the voice of Christ say, "Peace!"

Peace! and no longer from its brazen portals
The blast of War's great organ shakes the skies!
But beautiful as songs of the immortals,
The holy melodies of love arise.

NUREMBERG

In the valley of the Pegnitz, where across broad meadow-lands
Rise the blue Franconian mountains, Nuremberg, the ancient, stands.

Quaint old town of toil and traffic, quaint old town of art and song,
Memories haunt thy pointed gables, like the rooks that round them throng.

Memories of the Middle Ages, when the emperors, rough and bold,
Had their dwelling in thy castle, time-defying, centuries old;

And thy brave and thrifty burghers boasted, in their uncouth rhyme,
That their great imperial city stretched its hand through every clime.

In the court-yard of the castle, bound with many an iron band,
Stands the mighty linden planted by Queen Cunigunde's hand;

On the square the oriel window, where in old heroic days
Sat the poet Melchior singing Kaiser Maximilian's praise.

Everywhere I see around me rise the wondrous world of Art:
Fountains wrought with richest sculpture standing in the common mart;

And above cathedral doorways saints and bishops carved in stone,
By a former age commissioned as apostles to our own.

In the church of sainted Sebald sleeps enshrined his holy dust,
And in bronze the Twelve Apostles guard from age to age their trust;

In the church of sainted Lawrence stands a pix of sculpture rare,
Like the foamy sheaf of fountains, rising through the painted air.

Here, when Art was still religion, with a simple, reverent heart,
Lived and labored Albrecht Dürer, the Evangelist of Art;

Hence in silence and in sorrow, toiling still with busy hand,
Like an emigrant he wandered, seeking for the Better Land.

Emigravit is the inscription on the tombstone where he lies;
Dead he is not, —but departed,—for the artist never dies.

Fairer seems the ancient city, and the sunshine seems more fair,
That he once has trod its pavement, that he once has breathed its air!

Through these streets so broad and stately, these obscure and dismal lanes,
Walked of yore the Mastersingers, chanting rude poetic strains.

From remote and sunless suburbs came they to the friendly guild,
Building nests in Fame's great temple, as in spouts the swallows build.

As the weaver plied the shuttle, wove he too the mystic rhyme,
And the smith his iron measures hammered to the anvil's chime;

Thanking God, whose boundless wisdom makes the flowers of poesy bloom
In the forge's dust and cinders, in the tissues of the loom.

Here Hans Sachs, the cobbler-poet, laureate of the gentle craft,
Wisest of the Twelve Wise Masters, in huge folios sang and laughed.

But his house is now an ale-house, with a nicely sanded floor,
And a garland in the window, and his face above the door;

Painted by some humble artist, as in Adam Puschman's song,
As the old man gray and dove-like, with his great beard white and long.

And at night the swart mechanic comes to drown his cark and care,
Quaffing ale from pewter tankards; in the master's antique chair.

Vanished is the ancient splendor, and before my dreamy eye
Wave these mingled shapes and figures, like a faded tapestry.

Not thy Councils, not thy Kaisers, win for thee the world's regard;
But thy painter, Albrecht Dürer, and Hans Sachs thy cobbler-bard.

Thus, O Nuremberg, a wanderer from a region far away,
As he paced thy streets and court-yards, sang in thought his careless lay:

Gathering from the pavement's crevice, as a floweret of the soil,
The nobility of labor, —the long pedigree of toil.

THE NORMAN BARON

Dans les moments de la vie où la réflexion devient plus calme et plus profonde, où l'intérêt et l'avarice parlent moins haut que la raison, dans les instants de chagrin domestique, de maladie, et de péril de mort, les nobles se repentirent de posséder des serfs, comme d'une chose peu agréable à Dieu, qui avait créé tous les hommes à son image.

THIERRY: CONQUÊTE DE L'ANGLETERRE>

In his chamber, weak and dying,
Was the Norman baron lying;
Loud, without, the tempest thundered,
　　And the castle-turret shook,

In this fight was Death the gainer,
Spite of vassal and retainer,
And the lands his sires had plundered,
　　Written in the Doomsday Book.

By his bed a monk was seated,
Who in humble voice repeated
Many a prayer and pater-noster,
　　From the missal on his knee;

And, amid the tempest pealing,
Sounds of bells came faintly stealing,
Bells, that from the neighboring kloster
　　Rang for the Nativity.

In the hall, the serf and vassal
Held, that night, their Christmas wassail;
Many a carol, old and saintly,
　　Sang the minstrels and the waits;

And so loud these Saxon gleemen
Sang to slaves the songs of freemen,
That the storm was heard but faintly,
    Knocking at the castle-gates.

Till at length the lays they chanted
Reached the chamber terror-haunted,
Where the monk, with accents holy,
    Whispered at the baron's ear.

Tears upon his eyelids glistened,
As he paused awhile and listened,
And the dying baron slowly
    Turned his weary head to hear.

"Wassail for the kingly stranger
Born and cradled in a manger!
King, like David, priest, like Aaron,
    Christ is born to set us free!"

And the lightning showed the sainted
Figures on the casement painted,
And exclaimed the shuddering baron,
    "Miserere, Domine!"

In that hour of deep contrition
He beheld, with clearer vision,
Through all outward show and fashion,
    Justice, the Avenger, rise.

All the pomp of earth had vanished,
Falsehood and deceit were banished,
Reason spake more loud than passion,
    And the truth wore no disguise.

Every vassal of his banner,
Every serf born to his manor,
All those wronged and wretched creatures,
    By his hand were freed again.

And, as on the sacred missal
He recorded their dismissal,
Death relaxed his iron features,
    And the monk replied, "Amen!"

Many centuries have been numbered
Since in death the baron slumbered
By the convent's sculptured portal,
    Mingling with the common dust:

But the good deed, through the ages
Living in historic pages,
Brighter grows and gleams immortal,
    Unconsumed by moth or rust.

RAIN IN SUMMER

How beautiful is the rain!
After the dust and heat,
In the broad and fiery street,
In the narrow lane,
How beautiful is the rain!

How it clatters along the roofs,
Like the tramp of hoofs
How it gushes and struggles out
From the throat of the overflowing spout!
Across the window-pane
It pours and pours;
And swift and wide,
With a muddy tide,
Like a river down the gutter roars
The rain, the welcome rain!

The sick man from his chamber looks
At the twisted brooks;
He can feel the cool
Breath of each little pool;
His fevered brain
Grows calm again,
And he breathes a blessing on the rain.

From the neighboring school
Come the boys,
With more than their wonted noise
And commotion;
And down the wet streets
Sail their mimic fleets,
Till the treacherous pool
Ingulfs them in its whirling
And turbulent ocean.

In the country, on every side,
Where far and wide,
Like a leopard's tawny and spotted hide,
Stretches the plain,
To the dry grass and the drier grain
How welcome is the rain!

In the furrowed land
The toilsome and patient oxen stand;
Lifting the yoke encumbered head,
With their dilated nostrils spread,
They silently inhale
The clover-scented gale,
And the vapors that arise
From the well-watered and smoking soil.
For this rest in the furrow after toil
Their large and lustrous eyes
Seem to thank the Lord,
More than man's spoken word.

Near at hand,
From under the sheltering trees,
The farmer sees
His pastures, and his fields of grain,
As they bend their tops
To the numberless beating drops
Of the incessant rain.
He counts it as no sin
That he sees therein
Only his own thrift and gain.

These, and far more than these,
The Poet sees!
He can behold
Aquarius old
Walking the fenceless fields of air;
And from each ample fold
Of the clouds about him rolled
Scattering everywhere
The showery rain,
As the farmer scatters his grain.

He can behold
Things manifold
That have not yet been wholly told,—
Have not been wholly sung nor said.
For his thought, that never stops,
Follows the water-drops
Down to the graves of the dead,
Down through chasms and gulfs profound,

To the dreary fountain-head
Of lakes and rivers under ground;
And sees them, when the rain is done,
On the bridge of colors seven
Climbing up once more to heaven,
Opposite the setting sun.

Thus the Seer,
With vision clear,
Sees forms appear and disappear,
In the perpetual round of strange,
Mysterious change
From birth to death, from death to birth,
From earth to heaven, from heaven to earth;
Till glimpses more sublime
Of things, unseen before,
Unto his wondering eyes reveal
The Universe, as an immeasurable wheel
Turning forevermore
In the rapid and rushing river of Time.

TO A CHILD

Dear child! how radiant on thy mother's knee,
With merry-making eyes and jocund smiles,
Thou gazest at the painted tiles,
Whose figures grace,
With many a grotesque form and face.
The ancient chimney of thy nursery!
The lady with the gay macaw,
The dancing girl, the grave bashaw
With bearded lip and chin;
And, leaning idly o'er his gate,
Beneath the imperial fan of state,
The Chinese mandarin.

With what a look of proud command
Thou shakest in thy little hand
The coral rattle with its silver bells,
Making a merry tune!
Thousands of years in Indian seas
That coral grew, by slow degrees,
Until some deadly and wild monsoon
Dashed it on Coromandel's sand!
Those silver bells
Reposed of yore,
As shapeless ore,
Far down in the deep-sunken wells
Of darksome mines,
In some obscure and sunless place,
Beneath huge Chimborazo's base,
Or Potosi's o'erhanging pines
And thus for thee, O little child,

Through many a danger and escape,
The tall ships passed the stormy cape;
For thee in foreign lands remote,
Beneath a burning, tropic clime,
The Indian peasant, chasing the wild goat,
Himself as swift and wild,
In falling, clutched the frail arbute,
The fibres of whose shallow root,
Uplifted from the soil, betrayed
The silver veins beneath it laid,
The buried treasures of the miser, Time.

But, lo! thy door is left ajar!
Thou hearest footsteps from afar!
And, at the sound,
Thou turnest round
With quick and questioning eyes,
Like one, who, in a foreign land,
Beholds on every hand
Some source of wonder and surprise!
And, restlessly, impatiently,
Thou strivest, strugglest, to be free,

The four walls of thy nursery
Are now like prison walls to thee.
No more thy mother's smiles,
No more the painted tiles,
Delight thee, nor the playthings on the floor,
That won thy little, beating heart before;
Thou strugglest for the open door.

Through these once solitary halls
Thy pattering footstep falls.
The sound of thy merry voice
Makes the old walls
Jubilant, and they rejoice

With the joy of thy young heart,
O'er the light of whose gladness
No shadows of sadness
From the sombre background of memory start.

Once, ah, once, within these walls,
One whom memory oft recalls,
The Father of his Country, dwelt.
And yonder meadows broad and damp
The fires of the besieging camp
Encircled with a burning belt.
Up and down these echoing stairs,
Heavy with the weight of cares,
Sounded his majestic tread;
Yes, within this very room
Sat he in those hours of gloom,
Weary both in heart and head.

But what are these grave thoughts to thee?
Out, out! into the open air!
Thy only dream is liberty,
Thou carest little how or where.
I see thee eager at thy play,
Now shouting to the apples on the tree,
With cheeks as round and red as they;
And now among the yellow stalks,
Among the flowering shrubs and plants,
As restless as the bee.
Along the garden walks,
The tracks of thy small carriage-wheels I trace;
And see at every turn how they efface
Whole villages of sand-roofed tents,
That rise like golden domes
Above the cavernous and secret homes
Of wandering and nomadic tribes of ants.
Ah, cruel little Tamerlane,

Who, with thy dreadful reign,
Dost persecute and overwhelm
These hapless Troglodytes of thy realm!

What! tired already! with those suppliant looks,
And voice more beautiful than a poet's books,
Or murmuring sound of water as it flows,
Thou comest back to parley with repose;
This rustic seat in the old apple-tree,
With its o'erhanging golden canopy
Of leaves illuminate with autumnal hues,
And shining with the argent light of dews,
Shall for a season be our place of rest.
Beneath us, like an oriole's pendent nest,
From which the laughing birds have taken wing,
By thee abandoned, hangs thy vacant swing.
Dream-like the waters of the river gleam;
A sailless vessel drops adown the stream,
And like it, to a sea as wide and deep,
Thou driftest gently down the tides of sleep.

O child! O new-born denizen
Of life's great city! on thy head
The glory of the morn is shed,
Like a celestial benison!
Here at the portal thou dost stand,
And with thy little hand
Thou openest the mysterious gate
Into the future's undiscovered land.
I see its valves expand,
As at the touch of Fate!
Into those realms of love and hate,
Into that darkness blank and drear,
By some prophetic feeling taught,
I launch the bold, adventurous thought,
Freighted with hope and fear;

As upon subterranean streams,
In caverns unexplored and dark,
Men sometimes launch a fragile bark,
Laden with flickering fire,
And watch its swift-receding beams,
Until at length they disappear,
And in the distant dark expire.

By what astrology of fear or hope
Dare I to cast thy horoscope!
Like the new moon thy life appears;
A little strip of silver light,
And widening outward into night
The shadowy disk of future years;
And yet upon its outer rim,
A luminous circle, faint and dim,
And scarcely visible to us here,
Rounds and completes the perfect sphere;
A prophecy and intimation,
A pale and feeble adumbration,
Of the great world of light, that lies
Behind all human destinies.

Ah! if thy fate, with anguish fraught,
Should be to wet the dusty soil
With the hot tears and sweat of toil,—
To struggle with imperious thought,
Until the overburdened brain,
Weary with labor, faint with pain,
Like a jarred pendulum, retain
Only its motion, not its power,—
Remember, in that perilous hour,
When most afflicted and oppressed,
From labor there shall come forth rest.

And if a more auspicious fate
On thy advancing steps await
Still let it ever be thy pride
To linger by the laborer's side;
With words of sympathy or song
To cheer the dreary march along
Of the great army of the poor,
O'er desert sand, o'er dangerous moor.
Nor to thyself the task shall be
Without reward; for thou shalt learn
The wisdom early to discern
True beauty in utility;
As great Pythagoras of yore,
Standing beside the blacksmith's door,
And hearing the hammers, as they smote
The anvils with a different note,
Stole from the varying tones, that hung
Vibrant on every iron tongue,
The secret of the sounding wire.
And formed the seven-chorded lyre.

Enough! I will not play the Seer;
I will no longer strive to ope
The mystic volume, where appear
The herald Hope, forerunning Fear,
And Fear, the pursuivant of Hope.
Thy destiny remains untold;
For, like Acestes' shaft of old,
The swift thought kindles as it flies,
And burns to ashes in the skies.

THE OCCULTATION OF ORION

I saw, as in a dream sublime,
The balance in the hand of Time.
O'er East and West its beam impended;
And day, with all its hours of light,
Was slowly sinking out of sight,
While, opposite, the scale of night
Silently with the stars ascended.

Like the astrologers of eld,
In that bright vision I beheld
Greater and deeper mysteries.
I saw, with its celestial keys,
Its chords of air, its frets of fire,
The Samian's great Aeolian lyre,
Rising through all its sevenfold bars,
From earth unto the fixed stars.
And through the dewy atmosphere,
Not only could I see, but hear,
Its wondrous and harmonious strings,
In sweet vibration, sphere by sphere,
From Dian's circle light and near,
Onward to vaster and wider rings.
Where, chanting through his beard of snows,
Majestic, mournful, Saturn goes,
And down the sunless realms of space
Reverberates the thunder of his bass.

Beneath the sky's triumphal arch
This music sounded like a march,
And with its chorus seemed to be
Preluding some great tragedy.
Sirius was rising in the east;
And, slow ascending one by one,
The kindling constellations shone.
Begirt with many a blazing star,
Stood the great giant Algebar,
Orion, hunter of the beast!
His sword hung gleaming by his side,
And, on his arm, the lion's hide
Scattered across the midnight air
The golden radiance of its hair.

The moon was pallid, but not faint;
And beautiful as some fair saint,
Serenely moving on her way
In hours of trial and dismay.
As if she heard the voice of God,
Unharmed with naked feet she trod
Upon the hot and burning stars,
As on the glowing coals and bars,
That were to prove her strength, and try
Her holiness and her purity.

Thus moving on, with silent pace,
And triumph in her sweet, pale face,
She reached the station of Orion.
Aghast he stood in strange alarm!
And suddenly from his outstretched arm
Down fell the red skin of the lion
Into the river at his feet.
His mighty club no longer beat
The forehead of the bull; but he
Reeled as of yore beside the sea,

When, blinded by Oenopion,
He sought the blacksmith at his forge,
And, climbing up the mountain gorge,
Fixed his blank eyes upon the sun.

Then, through the silence overhead,
An angel with a trumpet said,
"Forevermore, forevermore,
The reign of violence is o'er!"
And, like an instrument that flings
Its music on another's strings,
The trumpet of the angel cast
Upon the heavenly lyre its blast,
And on from sphere to sphere the words
Re-echoed down the burning chords,--
"Forevermore, forevermore,
The reign of violence is o'er!"

THE BRIDGE

I stood on the bridge at midnight,
  As the clocks were striking the hour,
And the moon rose o'er the city,
  Behind the dark church-tower.

I saw her bright reflection
  In the waters under me,
Like a golden goblet falling
  And sinking into the sea.

And far in the hazy distance
  Of that lovely night in June,
The blaze of the flaming furnace
  Gleamed redder than the moon.

Among the long, black rafters
  The wavering shadows lay,
And the current that came from the ocean
  Seemed to lift and bear them away;

As, sweeping and eddying through them,
  Rose the belated tide,
And, streaming into the moonlight,
  The seaweed floated wide.

And like those waters rushing
  Among the wooden piers,
A flood of thoughts came o'er me
  That filled my eyes with tears.

How often, oh, how often,
In the days that had gone by,
I had stood on that bridge at midnight
And gazed on that wave and sky!

How often, oh, how often,
I had wished that the ebbing tide
Would bear me away on its bosom
O'er the ocean wild and wide!

For my heart was hot and restless,
And my life was full of care,
And the burden laid upon me
Seemed greater than I could bear.

But now it has fallen from me,
It is buried in the sea;
And only the sorrow of others
Throws its shadow over me.

Yet whenever I cross the river
On its bridge with wooden piers,
Like the odor of brine from the ocean
Comes the thought of other years.

And I think how many thousands
Of care-encumbered men,
Each bearing his burden of sorrow,
Have crossed the bridge since then.

I see the long procession
Still passing to and fro,
The young heart hot and restless,
And the old subdued and slow!

And forever and forever,
    As long as the river flows,
As long as the heart has passions,
    As long as life has woes;

The moon and its broken reflection
    And its shadows shall appear,
As the symbol of love in heaven,
    And its wavering image here.

TO THE DRIVING CLOUD

Gloomy and dark art thou, O chief of the mighty Omahas;
Gloomy and dark as the driving cloud, whose name thou hast taken!
Wrapped in thy scarlet blanket, I see thee stalk through the city's
Narrow and populous streets, as once by the margin of rivers
Stalked those birds unknown, that have left us only their footprints.
What, in a few short years, will remain of thy race but the footprints?

How canst thou walk these streets, who hast trod the green turf of the prairies!
How canst thou breathe this air, who hast breathed the sweet air of the mountains!
Ah! 'tis in vain that with lordly looks of disdain thou dost challenge
Looks of disdain in return, and question these walls and these pavements,
Claiming the soil for thy hunting-grounds, while down-trodden millions
Starve in the garrets of Europe, and cry from its caverns that they, too,
Have been created heirs of the earth, and claim its division!

Back, then, back to thy woods in the regions west of the Wabash!
There as a monarch thou reignest. In autumn the leaves of the maple
Pave the floors of thy palace-halls with gold, and in summer
Pine-trees waft through its chambers the odorous breath of their branches.
There thou art strong and great, a hero, a tamer of horses!
There thou chasest the stately stag on the banks of the Elkhorn,
Or by the roar of the Running-Water, or where the Omaha
Calls thee, and leaps through the wild ravine like a brave of the Blackfeet!

Hark! what murmurs arise from the heart of those mountainous deserts?
Is it the cry of the Foxes and Crows, or the mighty Behemoth,
Who, unharmed, on his tusks once caught the bolts of the thunder,
And now lurks in his lair to destroy the race of the red man?
Far more fatal to thee and thy race than the Crows and the Foxes,
Far more fatal to thee and thy race than the tread of Behemoth,
Lo! the big thunder-canoe, that steadily breasts the Missouri's
Merciless current! and yonder, afar on the prairies, the camp-fires
Gleam through the night; and the cloud of dust in the gray of the daybreak
Marks not the buffalo's track, nor the Mandan's dexterous horse-race;
It is a caravan, whitening the desert where dwell the Camanches!

Ha! how the breath of these Saxons and Celts, like the blast of the east-wind,
Drifts evermore to the west the scanty smokes of thy wigwams!

SONG

SEAWEED

When descends on the Atlantic
  The gigantic
Storm-wind of the equinox,
Landward in his wrath he scourges
  The toiling surges,
Laden with seaweed from the rocks:

From Bermuda's reefs; from edges
  Of sunken ledges,
In some far-off, bright Azore;
From Bahama, and the dashing,
  Silver-flashing
Surges of San Salvador;

From the tumbling surf, that buries
  The Orkneyan skerries,
Answering the hoarse Hebrides;
And from wrecks of ships, and drifting
  Spars, uplifting
On the desolate, rainy seas;—

Ever drifting, drifting, drifting
  On the shifting
Currents of the restless main;
Till in sheltered coves, and reaches
  Of sandy beaches,
All have found repose again.

So when storms of wild emotion
  Strike the ocean
Of the poet's soul, erelong
From each cave and rocky fastness,
  In its vastness,
Floats some fragment of a song:

Front the far-off isles enchanted,
  Heaven has planted
With the golden fruit of Truth;
From the flashing surf, whose vision
  Gleams Elysian
In the tropic clime of Youth;

From the strong Will, and the Endeavor
  That forever
Wrestle with the tides of Fate
From the wreck of Hopes far-scattered,
  Tempest-shattered,
Floating waste and desolate;—

Ever drifting, drifting, drifting
  On the shifting
Currents of the restless heart;
Till at length in books recorded,
  They, like hoarded
Household words, no more depart.

THE DAY IS DONE

The day is done, and the darkness
   Falls from the wings of Night,
As a feather is wafted downward
   From an eagle in his flight.

I see the lights of the village
   Gleam through the rain and the mist,
And a feeling of sadness comes o'er me
   That my soul cannot resist:

A feeling of sadness and longing,
   That is not akin to pain,
And resembles sorrow only
   As the mist resembles the rain.

Come, read to me some poem,
   Some simple and heartfelt lay,
That shall soothe this restless feeling,
   And banish the thoughts of day.

Not from the grand old masters,
   Not from the bards sublime,
Whose distant footsteps echo
   Through the corridors of Time.

For, like strains of martial music,
   Their mighty thoughts suggest
Life's endless toil and endeavor;
   And to-night I long for rest.

Read from some humbler poet,
Whose songs gushed from his heart,
As showers from the clouds of summer,
Or tears from the eyelids start;

Who, through long days of labor,
And nights devoid of ease,
Still heard in his soul the music
Of wonderful melodies.

Such songs have power to quiet
The restless pulse of care,
And come like the benediction
That follows after prayer.

Then read from the treasured volume
The poem of thy choice,
And lend to the rhyme of the poet
The beauty of thy voice.

And the night shall be filled with music
And the cares, that infest the day,
Shall fold their tents, like the Arabs,
And as silently steal away.

AFTERNOON IN FEBRUARY

The day is ending,
The night is descending;
The marsh is frozen,
  The river dead.

Through clouds like ashes
The red sun flashes
On village windows
  That glimmer red.

The snow recommences;
The buried fences
Mark no longer
  The road o'er the plain;

While through the meadows,
Like fearful shadows,
Slowly passes
  A funeral train.

The bell is pealing,
And every feeling
Within me responds
  To the dismal knell;

Shadows are trailing,
My heart is bewailing
And tolling within
  Like a funeral bell.

TO AN OLD DANISH SONG-BOOK

Welcome, my old friend,
Welcome to a foreign fireside,
While the sullen gales of autumn
Shake the windows.

The ungrateful world
Has, it seems, dealt harshly with thee,
Since, beneath the skies of Denmark,
First I met thee.

There are marks of age,
There are thumb-marks on thy margin,
Made by hands that clasped thee rudely,
At the alehouse.

Soiled and dull thou art;
Yellow are thy time-worn pages,
As the russet, rain-molested
Leaves of autumn.

Thou art stained with wine
Scattered from hilarious goblets,
As the leaves with the libations
Of Olympus.

Yet dost thou recall
Days departed, half-forgotten,
When in dreamy youth I wandered
By the Baltic,—

When I paused to hear
The old ballad of King Christian
Shouted from suburban taverns
In the twilight.

Thou recallest bards,
Who, in solitary chambers,
And with hearts by passion wasted,
Wrote thy pages.

Thou recallest homes
Where thy songs of love and friendship
Made the gloomy Northern winter
Bright as summer.

Once some ancient Scald,
In his bleak, ancestral Iceland,
Chanted staves of these old ballads
To the Vikings.

Once in Elsinore,
At the court of old King Hamlet
Yorick and his boon companions
Sang these ditties.

Once Prince Frederick's Guard
Sang them in their smoky barracks;—
Suddenly the English cannon
Joined the chorus!

Peasants in the field,
Sailors on the roaring ocean,
Students, tradesmen, pale mechanics,
All have sung them.

Thou hast been their friend;
They, alas! have left thee friendless!
Yet at least by one warm fireside
Art thou welcome.

And, as swallows build
In these wide, old-fashioned chimneys,
So thy twittering songs shall nestle
In my bosom,—

Quiet, close, and warm,
Sheltered from all molestation,
And recalling by their voices
Youth and travel.

WALTER VON DER VOGELWEIDE

Vogelweid the Minnesinger,
    When he left this world of ours,
Laid his body in the cloister,
    Under Wurtzburg's minster towers.

And he gave the monks his treasures,
    Gave them all with this behest:
They should feed the birds at noontide
    Daily on his place of rest;

Saying, "From these wandering minstrels
    I have learned the art of song;
Let me now repay the lessons
    They have taught so well and long."

Thus the bard of love departed;
    And, fulfilling his desire,
On his tomb the birds were feasted
    By the children of the choir.

Day by day, o'er tower and turret,
    In foul weather and in fair,
Day by day, in vaster numbers,
    Flocked the poets of the air.

On the tree whose heavy branches
    Overshadowed all the place,
On the pavement, on the tombstone,
    On the poet's sculptured face,

On the cross-bars of each window,
  On the lintel of each door,
They renewed the War of Wartburg,
  Which the bard had fought before.

There they sang their merry carols,
  Sang their lauds on every side;
And the name their voices uttered
  Was the name of Vogelweid.

Till at length the portly abbot
  Murmured, "Why this waste of food?
Be it changed to loaves henceforward
  For our fasting brotherhood."

Then in vain o'er tower and turret,
  From the walls and woodland nests,
When the minster bells rang noontide,
  Gathered the unwelcome guests.

Then in vain, with cries discordant,
  Clamorous round the Gothic spire,
Screamed the feathered Minnesingers
  For the children of the choir.

Time has long effaced the inscriptions
  On the cloister's funeral stones,
And tradition only tells us
  Where repose the poet's bones.

But around the vast cathedral,
  By sweet echoes multiplied,
Still the birds repeat the legend,
  And the name of Vogelweid.

DRINKING SONG

INSCRIPTION FOR AN ANTIQUE PITCHER

Come, old friend! sit down and listen!
From the pitcher, placed between us,
How the waters laugh and glisten
In the head of old Silenus!

Old Silenus, bloated, drunken,
Led by his inebriate Satyrs;
On his breast his head is sunken,
Vacantly he leers and chatters.

Fauns with youthful Bacchus follow;
Ivy crowns that brow supernal
As the forehead of Apollo,
And possessing youth eternal.

Round about him, fair Bacchantes,
Bearing cymbals, flutes, and thyrses,
Wild from Naxian groves, or Zante's
Vineyards, sing delirious verses.

Thus he won, through all the nations,
Bloodless victories, and the farmer
Bore, as trophies and oblations,
Vines for banners, ploughs for armor.

Judged by no o'erzealous rigor,
Much this mystic throng expresses:
Bacchus was the type of vigor,
And Silenus of excesses.

These are ancient ethnic revels,
    Of a faith long since forsaken;
Now the Satyrs, changed to devils,
    Frighten mortals wine-o'ertaken.

Now to rivulets from the mountains
    Point the rods of fortune-tellers;
Youth perpetual dwells in fountains,—
    Not in flasks, and casks, and cellars.

Claudius, though he sang of flagons
    And huge tankards filled with Rhenish,
From that fiery blood of dragons
    Never would his own replenish.

Even Redi, though he chaunted
    Bacchus in the Tuscan valleys,
Never drank the wine he vaunted
    In his dithyrambic sallies.

Then with water fill the pitcher
    Wreathed about with classic fables;
Ne'er Falernian threw a richer
    Light upon Lucullus' tables.

Come, old friend, sit down and listen
    As it passes thus between us,
How its wavelets laugh and glisten
    In the head of old Silenus!

THE OLD CLOCK ON THE STAIRS

L'éternité est une pendule, dont le balancier dit et redit sans cesse ces aeux mots seulement, dans le silence des tombeaux: "Toujours! jamais! Jamais! toujours!"

JACQUES BRIDAINE

Somewhat back from the village street
Stands the old-fashioned country-seat.
Across its antique portico
Tall poplar-trees their shadows throw;
And from its station in the hall
An ancient timepiece says to all,—
"Forever—never!
Never—forever!"

Half-way up the stairs it stands,
And points and beckons with its hands
From its case of massive oak,
Like a monk, who, under his cloak,
Crosses himself, and sighs, alas!
With sorrowful voice to all who pass,—
"Forever—never!
Never—forever!"

By day its voice is low and light;
But in the silent dead of night,
Distinct as a passing footstep's fall,
It echoes along the vacant hall,
Along the ceiling, along the floor,
And seems to say, at each chamber-door,—
"Forever—never!
Never—forever!"

Through days of sorrow and of mirth,
Through days of death and days of birth,
Through every swift vicissitude
Of changeful time, unchanged it has stood,
And as if, like God, it all things saw,
It calmly repeats those words of awe,—
"Forever—never!
Never—forever!"

In that mansion used to be
Free-hearted Hospitality;
His great fires up the chimney roared;
The stranger feasted at his board;
But, like the skeleton at the feast,
That warning timepiece never ceased,—
"Forever—never!
Never—forever!"

There groups of merry children played,
There youths and maidens dreaming strayed;
O precious hours! O golden prime,
And affluence of love and time!
Even as a Miser counts his gold,
Those hours the ancient timepiece told,—
"Forever—never!
Never—forever!"

From that chamber, clothed in white,
The bride came forth on her wedding night;
There, in that silent room below,
The dead lay in his shroud of snow;
And in the hush that followed the prayer,
Was heard the old clock on the stair,—
"Forever—never!
Never—forever!"

All are scattered now and fled,
Some are married, some are dead;
And when I ask, with throbs of pain.
"Ah! when shall they all meet again?"
As in the days long since gone by,
The ancient timepiece makes reply,—
    "Forever—never!
    Never—forever!"

Never here, forever there,
Where all parting, pain, and care,
And death, and time shall disappear,--
Forever there, but never here!
The horologe of Eternity
Sayeth this incessantly,—
    "Forever—never!
    Never—forever!"

THE ARROW AND THE SONG

I shot an arrow into the air,
It fell to earth, I knew not where;
For, so swiftly it flew, the sight
Could not follow it in its flight.

I breathed a song into the air,
It fell to earth, I knew not where;
For who has sight so keen and strong,
That it can follow the flight of song?

Long, long afterward, in an oak
I found the arrow, still unbroke;
And the song, from beginning to end,
I found again in the heart of a friend.

SONNETS

THE EVENING STAR

Lo! in the painted oriel of the West,
  Whose panes the sunken sun incarnadines,
  Like a fair lady at her casement, shines
  The evening star, the star of love and rest!
And then anon she doth herself divest
  Of all her radiant garments, and reclines
  Behind the sombre screen of yonder pines,
  With slumber and soft dreams of love oppressed.
O my beloved, my sweet Hesperus!
  My morning and my evening star of love!
  My best and gentlest lady! even thus,
As that fair planet in the sky above,
  Dost thou retire unto thy rest at night,
  And from thy darkened window fades the light.

AUTUMN

Thou comest, Autumn, heralded by the rain,
  With banners, by great gales incessant fanned,
  Brighter than brightest silks of Samarcand,
  And stately oxen harnessed to thy wain!
Thou standest, like imperial Charlemagne,
  Upon thy bridge of gold; thy royal hand
  Outstretched with benedictions o'er the land,
  Blessing the farms through all thy vast domain!
Thy shield is the red harvest moon, suspended
  So long beneath the heaven's o'erhanging eaves;
  Thy steps are by the farmer's prayers attended;
Like flames upon an altar shine the sheaves;
  And, following thee, in thy ovation splendid,
  Thine almoner, the wind, scatters the golden leaves!

DANTE

Tuscan, that wanderest through the realms of gloom,
  With thoughtful pace, and sad, majestic eyes,
  Stern thoughts and awful from thy soul arise,
  Like Farinata from his fiery tomb.
Thy sacred song is like the trump of doom;
  Yet in thy heart what human sympathies,
  What soft compassion glows, as in the skies
  The tender stars their clouded lamps relume!
Methinks I see thee stand, with pallid cheeks
  By Fra Hilario in his diocese,
  As up the convent-walls, in golden streaks,
The ascending sunbeams mark the day's decrease;
  And, as he asks what there the stranger seeks,
  Thy voice along the cloister whispers, "Peace!"

TRANSLATIONS

THE HEMLOCK-TREE

From the German

O HEMLOCK tree! O hemlock tree! how faithful are thy branches!
Green not alone in summer time,
But in the winter's frost and rime!
O hemlock tree! O hemlock tree! how faithful are thy branches!

O maiden fair! O maiden fair! how faithless is thy bosom !
To love me in prosperity,
And leave me in adversity!
O maiden fair! O maiden fair! how faithless is thy bosom!

The nightingale, the nightingale, thou tak'st for thine example!
So long as summer laughs she sings,
But in the autumn spreads her wings.
The nightingale, the nightingale, thou tak'st for thine example!

The meadow brook, the meadow brook, is mirror of thy falsehood!
It flows so long as falls the rain,
In drought its springs soon dry again.
The meadow brook, the meadow brook, is mirror of thy falsehood!

ANNIE OF THARAW

FROM THE LOW GERMAN OF SIMON DACH

ANNIE of Tharaw, my true love of old,
She is my life, and my goods, and my gold.

Annie of Tharaw, her heart once again
To me has surrendered in joy and in pain.

Annie of Tharaw, my riches, my good,
Thou, O my soul, my flesh and my blood!

Then come the wild weather, come sleet or come snow,
We will stand by each other, however it blow.

Oppression, and sickness, and sorrow, and pain
Shall be to our true love as links to the chain.

As the palm-tree standeth so straight and so tall,
The more the hail beats, and the more the rains fall,—

So love in our hearts shall grow mighty and strong,
Through crosses, through sorrows, through manifold wrong.

Shouldst thou be torn from me to wander alone
In a desolate land where the sun is scarce known,—

Through forests I'll follow, and where the sea flows,
Through ice, and through iron, through armies of foes.

Annie of Tharaw, my light and my sun,
The threads of our two lives are woven in one.

Whate'er I have bidden thee thou hast obeyed,
Whatever forbidden thou hast not gainsaid.

How in the turmoil of life can love stand,
Where there is not one heart, and one mouth, and one hand?

Some seek for dissension, and trouble, and strife;
Like a dog and a cat live such man and wife.

Annie of Tharaw, such is not our love;
Thou art my lambkin, my chick, and my dove.

Whate'er my desire is, in thine may be seen;
I am king of the household, and thou art its queen.

It is this, O my Annie, my heart's sweetest rest,
That makes of us twain but one soul in one breast.

This turns to a heaven the hut where we dwell;
While wrangling soon changes a home to a hell.

THE STATUE OVER THE CATHEDRAL DOOR

From the German of Julius Mosen.

FORMS of saints and kings are standing
The cathedral door above;
Yet I saw but one among them
Who hath soothed my soul with love.

In his mantle, —wound about him,
As their robes the sowers wind,—
Bore he swallows and their fledglings,
Flowers and weeds of every kind.

And so stands he calm and childlike,
High in wind and tempest wild;
O, were I like him exalted,
I would be like him, a child!

And my songs, —green leaves and blossoms,—
To the doors of heaven would bear,
Calling, even in storm and tempest,
Round me still these birds of air.

THE LEGEND OF THE CROSSBILL

From the German of Julius Mosen.

On the cross the dying Saviour
Heavenward lifts his eyelids calm,
Feels, but scarcely feels, a trembling
In his pierced and bleeding palm.

And by all the world forsaken,
Sees he how with zealous care
At the ruthless nail of iron
A little bird is striving there.

Stained with blood and never tiring,
With its beak it doth not cease,
From the cross 't would free the Saviour,
Its Creator's Son release.

And the Saviour speaks in mildness "
Blest be thou of all the good!
Bear, as token of this moment,
Marks of blood and holy rood!"

And that bird is called the crossbill;
Covered all with blood so clear,
In the groves of pine it singeth
Songs, like legends, strange to hear.

THE SEA HATH ITS PEARLS

From the German of Heinrich Heine.

THE sea hath its pearls,
  The heaven hath its stars;
But my heart, my heart,
  My heart hath its love.

Great are the sea and the heaven;
  Yet greater is my heart,
And fairer than pearls and stars
  Flashes and beams my love.

Thou little, youthful maiden,
  Come unto my great heart;
My heart, and the sea, and the heaven
  Are melting away with love!

POETIC APHORISMS

From the Sinngedichte of Friedrich von Logau.

Seventeenth Century.

MONEY.

WHEREUNTO is money good?
Who has it not wants hardihood,
Who has it has much trouble and care,
Who once has had it has despair.

THE BEST MEDICINES.

Joy and Temperance and Repose
Slam the door on the doctor's nose.

SIN.

Man-like is it to fall into sin,
Fiend-like is it to dwell therein,
Christ-like is it for sin to grieve,
God-like is it all sin to leave.

POVERTY AND BLINDNESS.

A blind man is a poor man, and blind a poor man is;
For the former seeth no man, and the latter no man sees.

LAW OF LIFE.

Live I, so live I,
To my Lord heartily,
To my Prince faithfully,
To my Neighbour honestly.
Die I, so die I.

CREEDS.

Lutheran, Popish, Calvinistic, all these creeds and doctrines three
Are extant; but still the doubt is, where Christianity may be.

THE RESTLESS HEART.

A millstone and the human heart are driven ever round;
If they have nothing else to grind, they must themselves be ground.

CHRISTIAN LOVE.

Whilom Love was like a fire, and warmth and comfort it bespoke ;
But, alas! it now is quenched, and only bites us, like the smoke.

ART AND TACT.

Intelligence and courtesy not always are combined;
Often in a wooden house a golden room we find.

RETRIBUTION.

Though the mills of God grind slowly, yet they grind exceeding small;
Though with patience he stands waiting, with exactness grinds he all.

TRUTH.

When by night the frogs are croaking, kindle but a torch's fire,
Ha! how soon they all are silent! Thus Truth silences the liar.

RHYMES.

If perhaps these rhymes of mine sound not well in strangers' ears,
They have only to bethink them that it happens so with theirs ;
For so long as words, like mortals, call a fatherland their own,
They will be most highly valued where they are best and longest known.

CURFEW

I.

Solemnly, mournfully,
  Dealing its dole,
The Curfew Bell
  Is beginning to toll.

Cover the embers,
  And put out the light;
Toil comes with the morning,
  And rest with the night.

Dark grow the windows,
  And quenched is the fire;
Sound fades into silence,—
  All footsteps retire.

No voice in the chambers,
  No sound in the hall!
Sleep and oblivion
  Reign over all!

II.

The book is completed,
  And closed, like the day;
And the hand that has written it
  Lays it away.

Dim grow its fancies;
  Forgotten they lie;
Like coals in the ashes,
  They darken and die.

Song sinks into silence,
  The story is told,
The windows are darkened,
  The hearth-stone is cold.

Darker and darker
  The black shadows fall;
Sleep and oblivion
  Reign over all.

NOTES

THE BELFRY OF BRUGES (p. 11)

"All the Foresters of Flanders."

THE title of Foresters was given to the early governors of Flanders, appointed by the kings of France. Lyderick du Bucq, in the days of Clotaire the Second, was the first of them; and Beaudoin Bras-de-Fer, who stole away the fair Judith, daughter of Charles the Bald, from the French court, and married her in Bruges, was the last. After him, the title of Forester was changed to that of Count. Philippe d'Alsace, Guy de Dampierre, and Louis de Crécy, coming later in the order of time, were therefore rather Counts than Foresters. Philippe went twice to the Holy Land as a Crusader, and died of the plague at St. Jeand'Acre, shortly after the capture of the city by the Christians. Guy de Dampierre died in the prison of Compiègne. Louis de Crécy was son and successor of Robert de Béthune, who strangled his wife, Yolande de Bourgogne, with the bridle of his horse, for having poisoned, at the age of eleven years, Charles, his son by his first wife, Blanche d'Anjou.

"Stately dames, like queens attended."

WHEN Philippe-le-Bel, king of France, visited Flanders with his queen, she was so astonished at the magnificence of the dames of Bruges, that she exclaimed: "Je croyais être seule reine ici, mais il paraît que ceux de Flandre qui se trouvent dans nos prisons sont tous des princes, car leurs femmes sont habillées comme des princesses et des reines."

When the burgomasters of Ghent, Bruges, and Ypres went to Paris to pay homage to King John, in 1351, they were received with great pomp and distinction; but, being invited to a festival, they observed that their seats at table were not furnished with cushions; whereupon, to make known their displeasure at this want of regard to their dignity, they folded their richly embroidered cloaks and seated themselves upon them. On rising from table, they left their cloaks behind them, and, being informed of their apparent forgetfulness, Simon van Eertrycke, burgomaster of Bruges, replied: "We Flemings are not in the habit of carrying away our cushions after dinner."

"Knights who bore the Fleece of Gold."

PHILIPPE DE BOURGOGNE, surnamed Le Bon, espoused Isabella of Portugal, on the 10th of January, 1430; and on the same day instituted the famous order of the Fleece of Gold.

"I beheld the gentle Mary."

MARIE DE VALOIS, Duchess of Burgundy, was left by the death of her father, Charles-le-Téméraire, at the age of twenty, the richest heiress of Europe. She came to Bruges, as Countess of Flanders, in 1477, and in the same year was married by proxy to the Archduke Maximilian. According to the custom of the time, the Duke of Bavaria, Maximilian's substitute, slept with the princess. They were both in complete dress, separated by a naked sword, and attended by four armed guards. Isabella was adored by her subjects for her gentleness and her many other virtues.

Maximilian was son of the Emperor Frederick the Third, and is the same person mentioned afterwards in the poem of Nuremberg as the Kaiser Maximilian, and the hero of Pfinzing's poem of Teuerdank. Having been imprisoned by the revolted burghers of Bruges, they refused to release him, till he consented to kneel in the public square, and to swear on the Holy Evangelists and the body of Saint Donatus, that he would not take vengeance upon them for their rebellion.

"The bloody battle of the Spurs of Gold."

THIS battle, the most memorable in Flemish history, was fought under the walls of Courtray, on the 11th of July, 1302, between the French and the Flemings, the former commanded by Robert, Comte d'Artois, and the latter by Guillaume de Juliers, and Jean, Comte de Namur. The French army was completely routed, with a loss of twenty thousand infantry and seven thousand cavalry; among whom were sixty-three princes, dukes, and counts, seven hundred lordsbanneret, and eleven hundred noblemen. The flower of the French nobility perished on that day; to which history has given the name of the Journée des Éperons d'Or, from the great number of golden spurs found on the field of battle. Seven hundred of them were hung up as a trophy in the church of Notre Dame de Courtray; and, as the cavaliers of that day wore but a single spur each, these vouched to God for the violent and bloody death of seven hundred of his creatures.

"Saw the fight at Minnewater."

WHEN the inhabitants of Bruges were digging a canal at Minnewater, to bring the waters of the Lys from Deynze to their city, they were attacked and routed by the citizens of Ghent, whose commerce would have been much injured by the canal. They were led by Jean Lyons, captain of a military company at Ghent, called the Chaperons Blancs. He had great sway over the turbulent populace, who, in those prosperous times of the city, gained an easy livelihood by laboring two or three days in the week, and had the remaining four or five to devote to public affairs. The fight at Minnewater was followed by open rebellion against Louis de Maele, the Count of Flanders and Protector of Bruges. His superb château of Wondelghem was pillaged and burnt; and the insurgents forced the gates of Bruges, and entered in triumph, with Lyons mounted at their head. A few days afterwards he died suddenly, perhaps by poison.

Meanwhile the insurgents received a check at the village of Nevèle; and two hundred of them perished in the church, which was burned by the count's orders. One of the chiefs, Jean de Lannoy, took refuge in the belfry.

From the summit of the tower he held forth his purse filled with gold, and begged for deliverance. It was in vain. His enemies cried to him from below to save himself as best he might; and, half suffocated with smoke and flame, he threw himself from the tower and perished at their feet. Peace was soon afterwards established, and the count retired to faithful Bruges.

"The Golden Dragon's nest."

THE Golden Dragon, taken from the church of St. Sophia, at Constantinople, in one of the Crusades, and placed on the belfry of Bruges, was afterwards transported to Ghent by Philip van Artevelde, and still adorns the belfry of that city.

The inscription on the alarm-bell at Ghent is, " Mynen naem is Roland; als ik klep is er brand, and als ik luy is er victorie in het land." My name is Roland; when I toll there is fire, and when I ring there is victory in the land.

NUREMBERG (p. 21)

"That their great imperial city stretched its hand through every clime."

An old popular proverb of the tower runs thus: —

"Nürnberg's Hand
Geht durch alle Land."
Nuremberg's hand
Goes through every land.

"Sat the poet Melchior singing Kaiser Maximilian's praise."

MELCHIOR PRINZING was one of the most celebrated German poets of the sixteenth century. The hero of his Teuerdank was the reigning emperor, Maximilian; and the poem was to the Germans of that day what the Orlando Furioso was to the Italians. Maximilian is mentioned before, in the Belfry of Bruges. See note to page 14.

"In the church of sainted Sebald sleeps enshrined his holy dust."

THE tomb of Saint Sebald, in the church which bears his name, is one of the richest works of art in Nuremberg. It is of bronze, and was cast by Peter Vischer and his sons, who labored upon it thirteen years. It is adorned with nearly one hundred figures, among which those of the Twelve Apostles are conspicuous for size and beauty.

"In the church of sainted Lawrence stands a pix of sculpture rare."

THIS pix, or tabernacle for the vessels of the sacrament, is by the hand of Adam Kraft. It is an exquisite piece of sculpture in white stone, and rises to the height of sixty-four feet. It stands in the choir, whose richly painted windows cover it with varied colors.

"Wisest of the Twelve Wise Masters."

THE Twelve Wise Masters was the title of the original corporation of the Mastersingers. Hans Sachs, the cobbler of Nuremberg, though not one of the original Twelve, was the most renowned of the Mastersingers, as well as the most voluminous. He flourished in the sixteenth century; and left behind him thirty-four folio volumes of manuscript, containing two hundred and eight plays, one thousand and seven hundred comic tales, and between four and five thousand lyric poems.

"As in Adam Puschman's song."

ADAM PUSCHMAN, in his poem on the death of Hans Sachs, describes him as he appeared in a vision:—

"An old man,
Gray and white, and dove-like,
Who had, in sooth, a great beard,
And read in a fair, great book,
Beautiful with golden clasps."

WALTER VON DER VOGELWEIDE. (p. 61)

WALTER VON DER VOGELWEIDE, or Bird-Meadow, was one of the principal Minnesingers of the thirteenth century. He triumphed over Heinrich von Ofterdingen in that poetic contest at the Wartburg Castle, known in literary history as the War of Wartburg.

AUTUMN. (p. 75)

"Like imperial Charlemagne."

CHARLEMAGNE may be called by preeminence the monarch of farmers. According to the German tradition, in seasons of great abundance, his spirit crosses the Rhine on a golden bridge at Bingen, and blesses the cornfields and the vineyards. During his lifetime, he did not disdain, says Montesquieu, "to sell the eggs from the farmyards of his domains, and the superfluous vegetables of his gardens; while he distributed among his people the wealth of the Lombards and the immense treasures of the Huns."

ABOUT THE AUTHOR

Henry Wadsworth Longfellow (1807-1882) was an American poet and educator. His best-known original works include "Paul Revere's Ride," "The Song of Hiawatha" and "Evangeline." He was the first American to completely translate Dante Alighieri's "Divine Comedy" and was one of the fireside poets from New England.

Longfellow wrote many lyric poems known for their musicality and often presenting stories of mythology and legend. He became the most popular American poet of his day and had success overseas. He has been criticized for imitating European styles and writing poetry that was too sentimental.

1807

—February 27, 1807: Birth of Henry Wadsworth Longfellow at Portland, Maine (which was at that time still part of Massachusetts). He was the son of Stephen Longfellow, a lawyer, and Zilch Wadsworth, daughter of Peleg Wadsworth, a general in the American Revolutionary War and a member of Congress. His mother was descended from Richard Warren, who was a passenger on the Mayflower. His Mayflower ancestors also included William Brewster and John and Priscilla Alden.

1810

—Longfellow att4ends a dame school at age three.
1812
—April 30: Louisiana becomes the 18th state to j
—June 18: The War of 1812 begins, during which the United States of America and its indigenous allies fought against the United Kingdom and its allies in British North America.

1813

—Longfellow is enrolled at age six at the private Portland Academy.
—A naval battle occurs between American and British sips offshore of New England. The treaty restored diplomatic relations and restored the pre-war borders of June 1812.

1814

—December 24: The Treaty of Ghent, a peace treaty concluding the War of 1812, was signed at Ghent, in the Netherlands, by representatives of the United States and the United Kingdom.

1816

—The statehood of Indiana is recognized, and Indiana becomes the 19th state of the Union. Indiana had previously been part of the Northwest Territory organized in 1787.

1817

—December 10: Mississippi becomes the 20th state admitted to the Union of the United States. Mississippi seceded from the Union and was restored to the Union in 1870, after the American Civil War.

1818

—Illinois achieved statehood after being part of the Northwest Territory for many years, becoming the 21st state of the Union.

1819

—December The statehood of Alabama is recognized. Alabama would later secede from the Union in 1861, rejoining the Union in 1868 after the American Civil War.

1820

—March 15: Maine becomes the 23rd state of the United States, as part of the Missouri Compromise, after residents voted to secede from the Commonwealth of Massachussets.
—Longfellow's first poem, "The Battle of Lovell's Pond," was published in the Portland Gazette on November 17, 1820. It was a patriotic and historical four-stanza poem.
—Nathaniel Hawthorne enrolls at Bowdoin College.

1821

—The former Missouri Territory is admitted to the Union as a slave state as part of the Missouri Compromise. Although the Confederacy recognized Missouri as its twelfth state, the secession was disputed and later regarded as not in effect.

1822

—Longfellow enrolls at Bowdoin College in Brunswick, Maine, along with his brother Stephen. His grandfather was a founder of the college and his father was a trustee. Here he met Nathaniel Hawthorne, a lifelong friend.

1824

—Nearly 40 minor poems by Longfellow are published between January 1824 and his graduation in 1825, many of these at the short-lived Boston periodical, The United States Literary Gazette."

1825

—Longfellow graduates from Bowdoin College, fourth in his class

and elected to Phi Beta Kappa. He gave the student commencement address.
—Longfellow is offered a job as professor of modern languages at his alma mater, on condition that he prepare by touring Europe and learning Romance languages.

1826

—January 30: Washington Irving, while living in Paris, is invited to travel to Madrid to inspect the Spanish archives in the library of the American consul.
—In May, Longfellow travels from New York to Le Havre, in France, aboard the ship 'Cadmus.' He spent three years in Europe, visiting France, Spain, Italy, Germany, and England. During his time abroad he learned French, Italian, Spanish, Portuguese, and German, mostly without formal instruction. While in Madrid, he met with Washington Irving, who encouraged his writing.
—July 4: Former U.S. Presidents Thomas Jefferson and John Adams both die on the 50th anniversary of the signing of the United States Declaration of Independence.

1827

—In the United Kingdom, George Canning succeeds Lord Liverpool as British prime minister.
—The term "socialist" is coined by Robert Owen in his London periodical, The Co-operative Magazine and Monthly Herald.

1828

—January: Washington Irving's book, "A History of the Life and Voyages of Christopher Columbus," was published.
—The first substantial praise of Longfellow's work is published, by John Neal, a fellow native of Portland, Maine, in the January 23, 1828 issue of his magazine, "The Yankee." He wrote: "As for Mr. Longfellow, he has a fine genius and a pure and safe taste,..."
—December 3: Andrew Jackson is elected President of the United States, defeating incumbent John Quincy Adams.

1829

—March 22; Greece receives autonomy from the Ottoman Empire.
—July 23: In the United States, William Burt obtains the first patent for a form of typewriter, the typographer.
—In mid-August, Longfellow returns to the United States.
—August 27: Longfellow wrote to the president of Bowdoin that he was turning down the professorship because he considered the $600 salary "disproportionate to the duties required." The trustees raised his salary to $800 with an additional $100 to serve as the college's librarian, which required one hour of work per day. While teaching at the college he translated textbooks from French, Italian, and Spanish.

1831

—July 21: Leopold of Saxe-Coburg-Gotha is inaugurated as the first King of the Belgians in Brussels.
—September 14, Longfellow marries Mary Storer, a childhood friend from Portland, Maine.

1832

—February 28: Charles Darwin and the crew of HMS Beagle arrive at South America for the first time.
—Greece is recognized as a sovereign nation by the Treaty of Constantinople, ending the Greek War of Independence.

1833

—Washington Irving's book, "Tales of the Alhambra," a book of short stories, is published.
—Longfellow's first published book was a translation of poetry by the medieval Spanish poet, Jorge Manrique, "Coplas de Don Jorge Manrique."
—Publication of several nonfiction and fiction prose pieces inspired by Irving, including "The Indian Summer" and "The Bald Eagle."

1834

—Longfellow receives a letter from Harvard College offering him the Smith Professorship of Modern Languages, with the stipulation that he spend a year abroad. He and his wife travel to Europe, where he studies German as well as Dutch, Danish, Swedish, Finnish, and Icelandic.
—The Spanish Inquisition, which had begun in the 15th century, is suppressed by royal decree.

1835

—Publication of "Outer-Mer: A Pilgrimage Beyond the Sea," a collection of Prose works by Longfellow. The term "outer-mer" is French for "overseas."
—September 7: Charles Darwin arrives at the Galapagos Islands, aboard HMS Beagle.
—November 29: Death of Longfellow's first wife, after a miscarriage. Her body was shipped home to the United States for burial at Mount Auburn Cemetery near Boston.
—December 28: The Second Seminole War led by Osceola breaks out.

1836

—Longfellow returns to the United States and assumes the professorship at Harvard.
—June 15: Arkansas is the 25th state admitted into the United States of America. Arkansas seceded from the Union in 1861 and rejoined in 186, after the American Civil War.
—Sam Houston is elected as the first president of the Republic of Texas.

1837

—January 26: Michigan becomes the 26th state of the United States, following the Toledo War, a boundary dispute with Ohio,

in which Ohio was granted the Toledo region and Michigan was given the western part of the Upper Peninsula.
—During the spring Longfellow has rented rooms at the Craigie House, built in 1759, which served as the headquarters of George Washington during the Siege of Boston. Previous boarders included Jared Sparks, Edward Everett, and Joseph Emerson Worcester. The house is preserved as the Longfellow House-Washington's Headquarters National Historic Site.
—Charles Dickens's "Oliver Twist" begins publication in serial form in London.

1838

—Longfellow writes the poem, "Footsteps of Angels," said to be about his late wife.
—June 28: The coronation of Queen Victoria takes place at Westminster Abbey in London.
—July 4: The Iowa Territory is formally established after a bill signed by U.S President Martin Van Buren on June 12.

1839

—Publication of Longfellow's first poetry collection, "Voices of the Night," his first book of poetry. Although most of the book was translations, it included nine original poems and seven poems that he had written as a teenager.
—During Longfellow's seven-year long courtship ofFrances "Fanny" Appleton, whose family lived at Beacon Hill in Boston. He often walked from Cambridge to the Appleton home by crossing the Boston Bridge. That bridge was replaced in 1906 with a new bridge later renamed as the Longfellow Bridge.
—Publication of "Hyperion: A Romance," a romance novel, whose main character, Paul Flemming, travels through Germany and falls in love with an Englishwoman who rejects him. The semi-autobiographical novel hints of his own travels, his atheistic beliefs and his own as yet unsuccessful courtship. The novel's descriptions of Germany would later inspire its use as a companion travel guide for American tourists in that country.

1840?

—Longfellow takes a six-month leave of absence from Harvard to attend a health spa in the former Marienberg Benedictine Convent at Boppard in Germany

1841

—Publication of Longfellow's "Ballads and Other Poems," which included "The Village Blacksmith" and "The Wreck of the Hesperus."
—January 26: Britain occupies Hong Kong, an island with a population of 7,500.
—March 4: William Henry Harrison is sworn in as the ninth President of the United States.
—April 6: John Tyler is sworn in as the tenth President of the United States, two days after Harrison's death of pneumonia.

1842

—Publication of the drama "The Spanish Student: A Paly in Three Acts," a play in which he reflects on his time in Spain in the 1820s.
—Publication of Longfellow's "Poems on Slavery," his first public support of abolitionism and anti-slavery efforts. Most of the poems were written at sea in October 1842. The poems were later reprinted as anti-slavery tracts in 1843, and included: "To William E. Channing," "The Slave's Dream," "The Good Part," "The Slave in the Dismal Swamp," "The Slave Singing at Midnight," "The Witnesses," "The Quadroon Girl," and "The Warning."

1843

—Longfellow marries Frances Elizabeth Appleton.
—Nathan Appleton, the father of Longfellow's wife, purchases the former Craigie house as a wedding present, and Longfellow lives there for the rest of his life.

1844

—Birth of Charles Appleton Longfellow
—Publication of "Poets and Poetry of Europe," with translations by Longfellow.

1845

—March 3: Florida is admitted to the Union as the 27th state. Florida, an area previously contested by Spain and Great Britain, had been ceded to the United States in 1819. Florida seceded from the Union in 1861 and rejoined in 1868, after the American Civil War.
—March 4: James K. Polk (1795-1849) is sworn in as the 11th president of the United States of America.
—Birth of Ernest Wadsworth Longfellow
—Publication of "The Belfry of Bruges and Other Poems," a poetry collection.
—Publication of "The Waif: A Collection of Poems," an anthology of poems by various authors, to which Longfellow contributed "Proem."
—December 29: Texas is recognized as the 28th state of the United States.

1846

—December 28, 1846: Iowa becomes the 29th state in the Union.

1847

—April 7: Birth of Fanny Longfellow, the Longfellows' first daughter. During childbirth, Dr. Nathan Cooley Keep administered ether to the mother as the first obstetric anestthetic in the United States.
—November 1: Publication of Longfellow's epic poem, "Evangeline: A Tale of Acadia."

1848

—May 29: Wisconsin becomes the 30th state to join the United States.

1849

—Publication of "Kavanagh: A Tale," a story of a country romance, in which Mr. Churchill, a school teacher, who has always planned to write a romance, but whose procrastination has never allowed him to start, until late in life he resigns himself to his "destiny."
—March 4: Major General Zachary Taylor (1784-1850) is sworn in as the 12th president of the United States of America.

1850

—Birth of Alice Mary Longfellow
—Publication of "The Seaside and the Fireside," a poetry collection.
—March 4: Millard Fillmore (1800-1874) is sworn in as the 13th president of the United States.

1851

—Publication of "The Golden Legend," a poem.

1852

—Publication of "The Poetical Works of Henry Wadsworth Longfellow," a poetry collection, in London, with illustrations by John Gilbert.

1853

—Birth of Edith Longfellow
—March 4: Franklin Pierce (1804-1869) is sworn in as the 14th president of the United States of America.
—June 13: Longfellow hosts a farewell dinner party at his Cambridge home for his friend Nathaniel Hawthorne., who was preparing to move overseas.

1854

—Longfellow retired from his teaching position at Harvard to focus on his writing

1855

—Birth of Anne Allegra Longfellow
—Publication of "The Song of Hiawatha," an epic poem in trochaic tetrameter, featuering Native American characters. The epic tells the fictional adventures of an Ojibwe warrior named Hiawatha and the tragedy of his love for Minnehaha, a Dakota woman.

1857

—March 4: James Buchanan (1791-1868) is sworn in as the 15th president of the United States of America.

1858

—May 11: The Minnesota Territory is admitted to the Union as the 32nd state in the United States.
—Publicaiton of "The Courtship of Miles Standish and Other Poems," a poetry collection. "The Coursthip of Miles Standish" is a narrative poem, written in dactylic hexameter, about the early days of Plymouth Colony, the colonial settlement established in America by the Mayfflower pilgrims. The poem was among the most enduringly popular of Longfellow's works.

1859

—February 14: Oregon is admitted to the Union as the 33rd state of the United States.
—Longfellow is awarded an honorary doctorate of laws from Harvard.

1860

—April 6: Longfellow writes the poem, "Paul Revere's Ride," commemorating the actions of Paul Revere on April 18, 1775, when he was said to warn American patriot defenders of the approaching British, although not a historically accurate account. It was written the day after Longfellow visited the Old North Church in Boston and climbed its tower It was first published in the January 1861 issue of 'The Atlantic Monthly.' Longfellow's family was said to have a connection to the historical Paul Revere in that his maternal grandfather, Peleg Wadsworth, had been Revere's commander during the Penobscot Expedition.

1861

—January 29: Kansas becomes the 39th state to join the United States.
—March 4: Abraham Lincoln (1809-1865) is sworn in as the 16th president of the United States of America.
—April 12: Start of the American Civil War, in which the Union states and the states of the southern Confederacy fought over issues of slavery.
—July 9: Longfellow's wife was sealing an envelope with hot sealing wax, or lighting a match, when her dress caught fire and her body was badly burned.
—July 10: Death of Francis Appleton, Longfellow's wife.
—Death of Longfellow's second wife, after sustaining burns when her dress caught fire. The distraught Longfellow was himself was injured by burns on his face, after trying to quench the flames with his body, and after that wore a beard to conceal the scars.

1863

—January 1: The Emancipation Proclamation was a presidential proclamation and executive order issued by Abraham Lincoln granted freedom to the slaves of the Confederacy.
—June 20: West Virginia is admitted to the Union as the 35th state of the United States, after seceding from the Confederate State of Virginia.
—July 1-3: The Battle of Gettysburg, fought near the town of Gettysburg in Pennsylvania, in which Union forces halted the Confederates' invasion to the north, was considered a turning point of the American Civil War.
—Publication of "The Legend of Rabbi Ben Levi," a poem telling about Yehoshua ben Levi, a Jewish rabbi and scholar of the Talmud

who lived in the land of Israel in the first half of the third century, and taught in the city of Lod, and was known for his debates of theological matters.
—November 23: Publication of "Tales of a Wayside Inn," a poetry collection, in whcih a group of people gathered at the Wayside Inn in Sudbury, Massachusetts, (about 20 miles from the poet's home in Cambridge), each take turns each telling a story in a variety of poetic forms and styles. The characters are said to be loosely based on actual persons of Longfellow's acquaintance. Includes his previously published poem, "Paul Revere's Ride," and "The Saga of King Olaf." Includes the "second flight" of "Bords of Passage").
—December 25: Longfellow writes the poem "Christmas Bells," which becomes the lyrics of the beloved Christmas carol, "I Heard the Bells on Christmas Day."

1864

—Longfellow launches the "Dante Club," of friends who meet weekly to help with perfecting the translation of Dante Alighieri's "Divine Comedy." Guests included regulars William Dean Howells, James Russell Lowell, and Charles Eliot Norton.
—October 31: Nevada becomes the 36th state of the Union.

1865

—Longfellow's poem, "Christmas Bells," is published in "Our Young Folks," a juvenile magazine published by Ticknor and Fields.
—Publication of "Household Poems," a poetry collection.
—April 9: Confederate General Robert E. Lee surrenders to Union General Ulysses S. Grant after the Battle of Appomattox Court House.
—April 15: Andrew Johnson (1808-1875) is sworn in as the 17th president of the United States of America, following the assassination of Abraham Lincoln.

1867

—March 1: Nebraska becomes the 37th state of the Union.
—Publication of "The Divine Comedy," Longfellows translation of

Dante Alighieri's work, in three volumes, although revisions continued and the work went through four printings in the first year.
—Publication of "Flower-de-Luce," a poetry collection.

1868

—Publication of "The New England Tragedies," containing two dramatic plays in verse reflecting on events in the early days of New England. The play "John Endicott" dramatizes the clash between the Puritans and the Quakers and the play "Giles Corey of the Salem Farms" is about the Salem witchcraft trials.

1869

—March 4: General Ulysses S. Grant (1822-1885) is sworn in as the 18th president of the United States of America.

1871

—Publication of Longfellow's translation of Dante Alighieri's "The Divine Tragedy," in three volumes.

1872

—Publication of "Christus: A Mystery," a trilogy composed of three previous works: "The Golden Legend," The New England Tragedies," and "The Divine Tragedy."
—Publication of "Three Books of Song," a poetry collection (including the second part of "Tales of a Wayside Inn").
—Longfellow's poem, "Christmas Bells," is set to music by the English organist, John Baptiste Calkin, using a melody called "Waltham." Other melodies have been used, including the 1845 melody of "Mainzer" and a 1956 tune by Johnny Marks, which was popularized by a Bing Crosby recording.

1873

—Publication of "Aftermath," (comprising the third part of "Tales of a Wayside Inn," and the "third flight" of "Birds of Passage").

1874

—Samuel Ward helped Longfellow with the selling of a poem, "The Hanging of the Crane," to the 'New York Ledger' for $3,000, the highest price ever paid for a poem.
—Longfellow oversees the publication of a 31-volume anthology, called "Poems of Places," which collected poems representing geographical locations, including European, Asian, and Arabian countries.

1875

—Publication of "The Masque of Pandora and Other Poems," a poetry collection.

1876

—August 1: Colorado is admitted to the Union, after being organized as the Territory of Colorado since 1861.

1877

—March 4: Rutherford B. Hayes (1822-1893) is sworn in as the 19th president of the United States of America.

1878

—Publication of "Kêramos and Other Poems," a poetry collection.

1880

—Publication of "Ultima Thule," a poetry collection.

1881

—March 4: James A. Garfield ((1831-1881) is sworn in as the 20th president of the United States of America.

1882

—March 24: Death of Longfellow at his home in Cambridge, surrounded by family. He is buried at Mount Auburn Cemetery in Cambridge, Massachusetts.
—Publication of "In the Harbor," a poetry collection.

—Publication of "Michael Angelo: A Frament," (incomplete, published posthumously).